Segundo Galilea

Temptation and Discernment

About the Author

Segundo Galilea is a priest of the archdiocese of Santiago, Chile, who has also worked extensively in the Philippines and North America. He is the author of numerous works in both Spanish and English, including The Future of Our Past *(Notre Dame, Indiana: Ave Maria Press, 1985), on the contemporary significance of Sts. John of the Cross, Ignatius of Loyola, and* Teresa of Avila.

Sources

Quotations from Ignatius of Loyola are taken from *The Spiritual Exercises of St. Ignatius,* trans. Louis J. Puhl (Westminster, Maryland: Newman Press, 1951), and are cited according to paragraph number.

Quotations from John of the Cross are taken from *The Collected Works of St. John of the Cross,* trans. Kieran Kavanaugh and Otilio Rodriguez, rev. ed. (Washington, DC: ICS Publications, 1991); texts from the *Ascent of Mount Carmel* and *Dark Night* are cited by book, chapter, and paragraph number, while excerpts from the *Spiritual Canticle* are cited by stanza and paragraph number.

Quotations from Teresa of Avila are taken from *The Collected Works of St. Teresa of Avila,* trans. Kieran Kavanaugh and Otilio Rodriguez, 3 vols. (Washington, DC: ICS Publications, 1976-1985); passages from the *Book of Her Life* are cited by chapter and section, while those from the *Interior Castle* are cited by "dwelling place," chapter, and section.

Segundo Galilea

Temptation and Discernment

Translated by Stephen-Joseph Ross, OCD

ICS Publications
Institute of Carmelite Studies
Washington, D.C.
1996

The original Spanish edition of this work was published under the title
Tentación y Discernimiento
by Centro de Espiritualidad Ignaciana in Chile
and is translated with their permission and that of the author.

ICS Publications
2131 Lincoln Road NE
Washington, DC 20002–1199

Typeset and produced in the U.S.A.
Cover design by Nancy Gurganus of Grey Coat Graphics.

Acknowledgments

An earlier version of parts of this translation appeared in the Summer 1991 issue of Spiritual Life *magazine.*

Scripture texts used in this work are taken from the *New American Bible* Copyright © 1991, 1986, and 1970 by the Confraternity of Christian Doctrine, Washington, DC 20017 and are used by permission of the copyright owner. All rights reserved. No part of the New American Bible may be reproduced in any form or by any means without permission in writing from the copyright owner.

Library of Congress Cataloging-in-Publication Data

Galilea, Segundo.
    [Tentación y discernimiento. English]
    Temptation and Discernment / Segundo Galilea;
translated by Stephen-Joseph Ross.
        p.   cm.
    ISBN: 0-935216-57-X
    1. Temptation. 2. Discernment of Spirits.
    3. Apostolate. (Christian theology) 4. Prayer—Christianity. I. Title.
BT725.G3513   1996
241'.4—dc20   96-11205
                                               CIP

TABLE OF CONTENTS

Introduction

Individuals or groups may find the following pages useful as an aid for a review of life or Christian spiritual discernment. The material examines and discerns what is good, what is defective, and above all what are the obvious and subtle temptations in two central areas of Christian life: prayer and ministry.

Prayer and ministry are central to the spirituality presented by the Gospel. These two privileged areas of life express the Christian experience of love of God and love of neighbor. Likewise they correspond to the two great poles of the human vocation—contemplation and action—which find their best synthesis in Christian spirituality.

The review of life proposed here begins with the most familiar temptations in today's world. The demons of these temptations are usually subtle and require discernment because they deal with Christian practices that in themselves are good. For that reason, a reflection on the nature of temptation, the devil's actions, and the discernment of spirits according to the great spiritual masters precedes the central themes of this study.

As a conclusion, we have added a brief reflection on discerning the Christian balance between renunciation and the search for happiness.

Part I

The Demons of Discernment

It is a mark of the evil spirit to assume the appearance of an angel of light. He begins by suggesting thoughts that are suited to a devout soul, and ends by suggesting his own. (Ignatius of Loyola, "Rules for the Discernment of Spirits, the Second Week," *Spiritual Exercises*, 332)

When the one who is giving the Exercises perceives that the exercitant is being assailed and tempted under the appearance of good, then is the proper time to explain...the rules of the Second Week [concerning discernment of spirits].... For commonly the enemy of our human nature tempts more under the appearance of good when one is exercising himself in the illuminative way. (Ignatius of Loyola, "Introductory Observations," *Spiritual Exercises*, 10).

PROLOGUE

Temptation is a normal part of human and Christian life. In itself it is not immoral nor does it imply any wrongdoing. It is only an invitation to some form of evil. Jesus himself also knew temptation, in a way compatible with his absolute holiness (although differently than we do, because the occasion of his temptation did not lie in his nature's tendencies but purely in the devil's action). From this it follows that no one is exempt from some type of temptation, not even one who has reached the highest levels of holiness. Wanting to have no temptations or to be free from certain ones is the additional temptation of subtle pride and angelism.

Temptation is commonly related to sin and the tendency to oppose deliberately the will of God who is our true good and happiness. People with a dependable and stable spirituality generally overcome the temptation to intentional evil without great difficulty. They recognize where the evil lies and usually have enough spirit to reject it.

However, the invitation to a mediocre Christian life is also a temptation. This form of temptation is characteristic of people who are already spiritual. Mediocrity, tepidity, and stagnation are not necessarily tied to one particular sin or another, or to a deliberate consent to evil, although with time they can lead to this. Neither is temptation to mediocrity explicitly perceived. It is a subtle temptation. At first it does not look like temptation, but instead it appears neutral or even good. What the person does or doesn't do, the way it is done, and one's habitual attitudes appear normal and reasonable. Nevertheless, people who have fallen into the temptation of mediocrity, tepidity, and stagnation do not experience true Christian fervor or progress. Faith, hope, love for God, prayer, fraternal charity, and ministry have become set in mediocrity.

The well-known text of the Book of Revelation refers to this kind of demon:

> I know your works; I know that you are neither cold nor hot. I wish you were either cold or hot. So, because you are lukewarm, neither hot nor cold, I will spit you out of my mouth. For you say, "I am rich and affluent and have no need of anything," and yet you do not realize that you are wretched, pitiable, poor, blind, and naked. I advise you to buy from me gold refined by fire so that you may be rich, and white garments to put on so that your shameful nakedness may not be exposed, and buy ointment to smear on your eyes so that you may see. Those whom I love, I reprove and chastise. Be earnest, therefore, and repent. (Rev 3:15-19)

The temptation to mediocrity, though seldom part of our awareness due to its complexity and subtlety, needs to be exposed, illuminated, and identified in order to be overcome. In short, it requires discernment. The salve that God offers in the scripture passage—"to smear on your eyes so that you may see"—corresponds to this act of discernment.

TEMPTATION AND SPIRITUAL DISCERNMENT
(ST. IGNATIUS AND ST. JOHN OF THE CROSS)

The practice of discernment is as old as Christian spirituality. To discern is to distinguish between good and evil in order to choose the good. It is to identify God's will in order to follow it. In this sense, discernment is applicable to all believers, whether their spiritual life is already profound or only in its beginning stages. In this general form, one often practices discernment instinctively according to the light of one's conscience.

There is, nevertheless, a more specific form of discernment, particularly applicable to our concern here with the subtle, deceitful temptations that lead to mediocrity. Tradition calls it "discernment of spirits." Here it is not so much a matter of distinguishing the explicitly evil from the good, but of differentiating the good spirit from the bad spirit; that is, discerning what is a call from God and what is temptation. Even with good will, the spiritual person easily confuses the two spirits. On this level, when we are dealing with spiritual people, the temptations are subtle; at first glance they do not seem bad and could even be taken as inspirations from God.

The discernment of spirits is much more complex than any other type of discernment. It requires experience, sound doctrine, and counsel. This discernment has a long tradition in Christian spirituality. It is present in varying degrees in the teaching of all the great mystics and spiritual masters, beginning with the desert fathers and mothers. However, not all of them attempted to analyze the subject in a systematic way, nor did all excel as teachers in the discernment of spirits.

Among the masters, the most well known and influential are Saint Ignatius of Loyola and Saint John of the Cross. Since these two, little new has been said about spiritual discernment. Their teaching inspired the following reflections.

Ignatius and John of the Cross complement one another, but the character of their mysticism differs. Ignatian mysticism is oriented towards apostolic service. His discernment seeks to arrive at some form of commitment, of "making a choice (*elección*) to serve Christ" in his church. (Making a choice is essential in Ignatian discernment and the key to his *Exercises*.) On the other hand, Sanjuanist mysticism is oriented to communion with God and neighbor through faith, hope, and love. John of the Cross is a contemplative mystic. His discernment is directed not so much toward orienting and confirming a way of making a choice for Christ, as it is toward purifying and bringing to maturity a choice already made. Thus the differences and the complementarity. Ignatius is more universal. In principle his *Spiritual Exercises* are appropriate for all who want to reform their lives; his doctrine of discernment is as suitable for those who want to begin to follow Christ as for those advanced in spirituality. John of the Cross speaks to those who are already on the way of Christian perfection. He assumes the first conversion and choice of a way of life. In fact, he directs most of his writings to members of the reformed Carmel. To be sure, his doctrine is universal; in principle, though, his writings are not as suitable for those who are just beginning, and even less so for those who require a first conversion.

Nevertheless, both mystics have the same objective: a discernment of spirits that allows the soul to adopt attitudes and make decisions leading toward a greater surrender to God through love. Both mystics, likewise, present discernment as a process of illumination that purifies and confirms one's capacity for loving and serving God. Their methods of explaining the process and doctrine of discernment differ because their writings are of two distinct types. The *Exercises* of Ignatius are schematic aids for the director, while the major prose writings of John are treatises. Ignatius proposes a system of "Rules" in pedagogical order (fourteen in the First Week of the *Exercises* and eight in the Second), in addition to the "times and ways of making a choice of a way of life" that characterize the Second Week and add valuable criteria for discerning the will of God. In contrast, John of the Cross's doctrine of discernment is not synthesized as such, but scattered throughout his writings, above all in his treatise *The Dark Night,* as he analyzes the subtle defects and temptations of "spiritual people." With implications for a process of discernment, the Carmelite saint's "nights" correspond to the illumination and painful purification of inordinate attachments. (John's "night," however, coincides with the Ignatian "desolation" only in some aspects, as we shall see later.)

In the end, both mystics also concur in the fact that their teaching on the discernment of spirits proceeds primarily from their personal experience. In this, Ignatius is particularly transparent. His rules for discernment and moments of making a choice correspond to his personal life experiences, historically identifiable during the first stages of his conversion of life.

CRITERIA FOR DISCERNING TEMPTATIONS

The criteria of both mystics for discerning what comes from God and what is temptation agree to a great extent, although their ways of explaining them are different. Both add original contributions that enrich and mutually complement one another. Ignatius explicitly identifies these criteria of discernment in the book of the *Exercises.* In John of the Cross, they are present throughout all his writings in a more implicit way. (He almost never uses the term "discernment," for example.)

In any case, they both agree on a fundamental criterion: **discerning the good spirit from the bad (temptation) requires a predisposition of interior freedom**, a progressive interior liberation from sins and deliberate faults, from inordinate affections and attachments, and from passions and tendencies that generally obscure and condition discernment. This interior freedom corresponds to the "indifference" of Ignatius and the "nothings" (*nadas*) of John of the Cross.

One of the foundations of the Ignatian *Exercises* is the grace of interior freedom to be able to respond with love and perseverance to the choice that God is requesting. (In the "Introductory Observations" [1], for example, he writes: "For, just as taking a walk, journeying on foot, and running are bodily exercises, so we call Spiritual Exercises every way of preparing and disposing the soul to rid itself of all inordinate attachments and, after their removal, of seeking and finding the will of God in the disposition of our life for the salvation of our soul." The same theme appears in number 23, "First Principle and Foundation.") Again, in his counsels for making "a good and correct choice of a way of life" (Second Week), Ignatius seeks to ensure interior freedom, as well as a holy objectivity and indifference, during times of making a choice. (See in the *Spiritual Exercises* the second point of the "way of making a choice," [179]; and the four rules that follow [184-187].)

John of the Cross follows another method on the road to this interior freedom. He analyzes the subtle and often unconscious temptations and enslavements of the soul that hinder spiritual people from greater freedom to love. At the same time he proposes how the soul should behave to receive enlightenment from God, and thus discern and purify this subtle servitude. Whereas Ignatius emphasizes making a choice for God's service, John of the Cross highlights communion with God. These are the two complementary dimensions of Christian mysticism. We read in the first book of the *Dark Night* (Chapters 2 to 7) that the characteristic quality of these imperfections and temptations is that spiritual persons do not perceive them as such. On the contrary, they seem to be doing well. The Carmelite saint sees in this a typical form of the deceitful influence of the devil. This can lead to a secret spiritual pride and complacency in practicing the Christian faith, or perhaps an increasing desire to delight in pleasurable sensory experiences, searching for gratification or wanting to appear spiritual before others. One may become discouraged and irritable when he or she does not "feel" spiritual fervor. There may be the tendency to compare oneself with others. For John of the Cross, discernment and the overcoming of these temptations that threaten interior freedom require God's purifying or illuminating action in the soul (the nights of the senses and of the spirit).

The two mystics likewise agree on another fundamental criterion: **the most subtle and dangerous temptation in spiritual persons is that which occurs under the appearance of good.** By this means, the devil deceives and obscures discernment. Thus in the fourth rule of the Second Week, Ignatius writes: "It is a mark of of the evil spirit to take on the appearance of an angel of light. He begins by suggesting thoughts that are suited to a devout soul.... Afterwards, he will endeavor little by little to end by drawing the soul into his hidden snares and evil designs" (*Spiritual Exercises*, 332). John of the Cross says: "It should be noted that among the many wiles of the devil for deceiving spiritual persons, the most common is deceiving them under the appearance of good rather than of evil, for the devil already knows that they will scarcely choose a recognized evil" (*Precautions*, 10).

This underscores the importance of taking into account other more particular criteria pertaining to the discernment of spirits.

Among these, **the criterion of "consolation-desolation"** occupies an eminent place in Ignatius's doctrine. In one way or another, this criterion is present in almost all the "rules for the discernment of spirits," whether in the First Week or the Second. The criterion is essentially this: What comes from God causes consolation in the soul; what comes from the evil spirit, from temptation, causes desolation. Consolation is peace, inspiration toward the good, intensity of faith, confidence in and love for God. These signs of consolation are not always accompanied by relief felt in the senses. What gives consolation is not necessarily what the person likes most. Interior aridity and sacrifice at times can accompany peace and inspiration toward the good. On the other hand, desolation is the condition contrary to consolation: confusion, anxiety, sadness, lukewarmness, etc. Likewise, sensory pleasure sometimes accompanies the signs of desolation. Desolation as well as consolation are experiences rooted in the depths of the soul, not in perceptions of the senses.

On this same topic, John of the Cross takes a different but converging path that complements Ignatius. His point of departure is not consolation-desolation in the process of spiritual discernment, but rather the **"nights"** and **"the aridity and trials of the dark night of the soul."** For John of the Cross, the night is essentially the presence of God's actions, a process in which the soul, in spite of everything, must keep itself faithful and at peace. (In this sense the night has affinities with Ignatian consolation and not with desolation.) The night is an experience of profound purification of spirit through aridity and trials. In his doctrine, the Carmelite saint seeks to help souls discern if this experience of the night is accomplishing the sanctifying end that God requires of it, or if the devil is taking advantage of aridity to make these persons believe they are evil because they do not "feel" the things of God, and thereby lead the soul to discouragement and mediocrity. John's goal is to discern if the night is rooted in consolation or moving toward desolation, to use Ignatian language. John of the Cross's criteria for discerning if one is in the night that comes from God or in the desolation of the evil spirit are twofold. In the night from God, one maintains the fundamental choice and faithfulness to God in all aspects of practicing the

Christian life. In the desolation from the evil spirit, faithfulness progressively declines. In the night there is no sensible consolation, but there is fidelity. What is important is not what one feels, but what one does (see especially *Ascent,* Prologue, 6).

> With divine help we will discuss all this: how individuals should behave; what method the confessor should use in dealing with them; signs to recognize this purification of the soul that we call the dark night; whether it is the purification of the senses or of the spirit; and how we can discern if this affliction is caused by melancholia or some other deficiency of sense or spirit.
>
> Some souls—or their confessors—may think that God is leading them along this road of the dark night of spiritual purgation, but perhaps this will not be so. What they suffer will be due to one of these deficiencies. Likewise, many individuals think they are not praying when, indeed, their prayer is deep. Others place high value on their prayer while it amounts to little more than nothing.

It can happen as well that at the beginning the evil spirit disguises himself with consolation and by that means leads the soul to desolation. Ignatius and John both approach these cases with a similar criterion of discernment: **The way to discern true or false consolation is by the fruits that ultimately prevail in the soul, and whether or not they belong to the spirit of God.**

Ignatius in the third and fifth rules of the Second Week insists: "both the good angel and the evil spirit can give consolation to a soul, but for a quite different purpose. The good angel consoles for the progress of the soul, that it may advance and rise to what is more perfect. The evil spirit consoles for purposes that are contrary, and that afterwards he might draw the soul to his own perverse intentions and wickedness.... It may end in what weakens the soul, or disquiets it; or by destroying the peace, tranquillity, and quiet which it had before...." (*Spiritual Exercises,* 331 and 333). John of the Cross notes that the communications that appear devout but come from the evil spirit "cause in the spirit agitation, or dryness, or vanity, or presumption. Yet diabolical communications are not as efficacious in doing harm as God's communications are in doing good. For the diabolical communications can only arouse the first movements without being able to move the will any further if it is unwilling to be moved.... The communications from God, however, penetrate the soul, move the will to love, and leave their effect within" (*Ascent*, 2, 11, 6). Thus the complementary thought of the two saints is evident again in the doctrine of discernment of consolation, desolation, and the nights.

There is one last basic criterion on which both saints agree: **Because of the deceitful nature of temptation and our lack of interior freedom, personal discernment often runs the risk of error even in using the traditional criteria. Therefore, in the process of discerning matters of evident importance, one must consult with competent people and ask their advice.** At the same time, this helps individuals confirm for themselves the course taken and the decisions made, which is very important for Ignatius. John of the Cross says: "It should be noted that among the many wiles of the devil for deceiving spiritual persons, the most common is deceiving them under the appearance of good.... To do the right thing, and be safe in such a matter, you ought to take the proper counsel" (*Precautions*, 10). Ignatius agrees: "When the enemy of our human nature tempts a just soul with his wiles and seductions, he earnestly desires that they be received secretly and kept secret. But if one manifests them to a confessor, or to some other spiritual person who understands his deceits and malicious designs, the evil one is very much vexed. For he knows that he cannot succeed in his evil undertaking, once his evident deceits have been revealed" ("Rules for the Discernment of Spirits," The First Week, *Spiritual Exercises*, 326).

This last criterion is **ecclesial**: it means having recourse in the discernment process to people who represent the church for us. This perspective later will lead Ignatius to write his "Rules for Thinking with the Church."

In summary, for Ignatius and John of the Cross the discernment of temptations characteristic of spiritual people is equivalent to discerning the good from the evil spirit. As a fundamental condition, both insist on interior freedom from disordered attachments of the will—"indifference" for the Jesuit and the *nada* (nothing) for the Carmelite. Presupposing this freedom, both adopt the basic criterion of consolation-desolation (understood as permanent and profound states of the soul and not merely transitory and purely sensible) as signs of the good and evil spirit respectively. Both stress the importance of verifying what one discerns with competent spiritual people to confirm the discernment and avoid the dangers of subjectivism.

Part II
The Demons of Ministry

Let those, then, who are singularly active, who think they can win the world with their preaching and exterior works, observe here that they would profit the Church and please God much more, not to mention the good example they would give, were they to spend at least half of this time with God in prayer.... They would then certainly accomplish more, and with less labor, by one work than they otherwise would by a thousand. For through their prayer they would merit this result, and themselves be spiritually strengthened. Without prayer they would do a great deal of hammering but accomplish little, and sometimes nothing, and even at times cause harm. (John of the Cross, *Spiritual Canticle*, 29, 3)

PROLOGUE

A good professional practice requires effective knowledgeable competence. The professional person's values and attitudes should also give the service a human character, making it acceptable to the recipients.

A doctor must be competent. An incompetent one cannot serve the health care profession with an effective practice. A doctor also requires certain spiritual qualities and attitudes to be successful. The medic must instill confidence, be available to the sick person, have common sense, keep confidentiality, etc. This collection of values gives form to what Christian language would express as the "spirituality" of a doctor.

Ministry (the "apostolic profession") requires analogous conditions: competence and use of pertinent methods, knowledge of certain subject matters and topics, and transmission of an appropriate message, to name a few. Likewise it requires the minister to have certain spiritual attitudes, convictions, and values. This is what, strictly speaking, constitutes the "spirituality of ministry."

On this point, however, ministry by its very nature is different from any other profession or activity, because its spirituality is essential for its effectiveness. **The attitude of the minister is a necessary condition for the fruit of his or her ministry.**

A very competent doctor with a mediocre spirit and ethics can be successful and heal patients. A minister with little spirit, though, usually does not have profound or decisive results and is only apparently successful. (We say "usually does not have" because God's grace may accomplish much good through a mediocre servant.) Here the spirit is more necessary than the ability.

Why is this so? Fundamentally ministry is God's "profession" made flesh, and not a human occupation. Its aim is to transmit God's way, truth, and life, and not those of human beings. For that reason Jesus Christ is the only minister, and men and women are ministers insofar as Jesus calls them to service and confers his power on them.

The spirit and values of God's ministers come totally and uniquely from the relationship of these men and women with Christ as his chosen ones, his messengers, and his instruments. Though free, they depend at the same time on the ministerial power of God. So each attitude, value, and conviction that shapes the spirituality of ministry is born from God.

We find these values in Jesus as the model and source, and in the saints through their imitation of Christ. In those who are not yet saints, we find them mixed with multiple inconsistencies, and with temptations that are more or less accepted. For that reason, one way of knowing the good spirit of ministry is knowing the inconsistencies and the temptations to which this service is subjected. The good spirit stands out in contrast to the evil spirit, and virtue is better known by knowing the "demons" that tempt it.

Let's see some of the more common "demons" of ministry. Experience, evaluated according to the Christian ideal of ministry, helps us to recognize them. The temptations reveal this ideal to us through contrast, in the same way shadows reveal light.

MESSIANISM

The demon of messianism leads ministers to set themselves up as the center of all pastoral activity in which they participate. The temptation subtly penetrates their lives, until they end up feeling indispensable in everything.

Messianism constitutes a faulty attitude concerning God: "I am the pilot, and the Lord is the assisting copilot." Those who fall into this temptation do not ignore God nor do they fail to pray and appeal to the Lord with problems. They do so, however, so that God may help them in the ministry they plan and direct. Ultimately, what we are dealing with here is incorporating the Lord into our work, and not incorporating ourselves into the work of God. Following the temptation, we unconsciously substitute our personal messianism for the messianic ministry of Christ, the one evangelizer.

This attitude before God manifests itself in an equally faulty attitude toward those with whom we collaborate. We become incapable of delegating responsibilities or tasks. We do not really trust people, except for a few—those who are a consistently faithful copy of ourselves, with whom we have permanently surround ourselves. Over the course of the years, this tendency generally becomes more and more pronounced.

There is always a relationship between the attitude towards God and the attitude towards others, and vice versa. Distrust of collaborators in ministry, therefore, reflects a distrust in God. This is what we mean by the demon of messianism. Trusting in God indeed assumes prudent confidence in others. This trust in others implies confidence in God who has called them and given them the position of companions in ministry.

Besides endangering the important fruit of evangelization, messianism has long-term negative consequences in other external ministerial endeavors. The messianic attitude does not allow others to grow, since the apostolic endeavor's growth and maturity do not run parallel as they should with the maturation and growth of all who carry it out. In the same way, the messianic ministers' initiatives and creations do not necessarily contribute to a community's formation nor do they prepare anyone to succeed them in ministry. Often they identify themselves with their work even to the point that the ministry ends when they leave or are transferred. It has been tied too much to the person, and successors are not prepared to step in.

True ministry, which has its origins in the church and builds the kingdom of God where it is not yet established, always contributes to the church's development. It forms its evangelizers and communities. One learns to be a Christian by learning to evangelize, and that is not possible without in fact taking on responsibilities. A mature minister reveals, among other things, that someone trusted in him or her.

ACTIVISM

The demon of activism is not the same as being very active or a hard worker, or having many jobs and various ministries. Being active as a minister is not falling into "activism" as a temptation.

Activism comes about insofar as it increases the distance and inconsistency between what ministers do and say, between who they are and how they live as Christians. In the human condition we do accept as normal some incompatibility between "being" and "doing." In the case of activism, though, the incongruity is intensified and tends to grow and not to diminish (as would be ideal in the Christian process).

Activism has many expressions. One of them is lack of renewal in the minister's personal life. In a systematic way, prayer is inadequate and poor. There are no prolonged periods of solitude and retreat. The minister does not cultivate study and seldom reads. One does not set aside time to rest sufficiently and recover. Similarly, one has an overload of work and multiple activities, and has packed the appointment book. Activists give the impression that a large volume of exterior work is necessary for their lifestyle. Excessive activity or neglect of renewal creates a vicious circle. The increase in activity makes it increasingly difficult to take measures for interior renewal that lead to growth in "being." On the other hand, the increasing incapacity for renewing oneself tends to be compensated for and disguised by surrendering to uncontrollable activity. In the end, activism is the excuse for "escapism."

Activism also expresses itself in one of the most radical distortions of ministry: putting one's entire soul into the means of organizing and doing the action of ministry, while at the same time forgetting God who is its source. The Lord is the one who organizes and accomplishes all things. Activist ministers transform themselves into professionals who multiply initiatives—all of them usually good.

They do not stop to discern or ask God if the undertakings are necessary, appropriate, or if they need to do them at the present time and in a particular way. The means of the apostolate have overshadowed its purpose and aim.

Not working in rhythm with God, but substituting one's tempo, is another expression of the demon of activism. That can occur when one goes faster or more slowly than God. The activist usually sins by going too fast, at least in the beginning. This arises from the lack of proportion that always exists between vision and ministerial projects, and the reality of the persons involved. Pastoral ministers normally have a greater vision than their community and people. They know beforehand and are more familiar with where and how they should do a particular project. The community does not respond to the tempo that these pastoral ministers would like, since its rhythm of growth corresponds to God's timing and not to the ministers' foresight. God's rhythm is a constant but slow process. Human beings (like plants and the rest of creation) do not change or grow with starts and stops, artificially skipping stages. We must wait and be patient, without ceasing to educate, cultivate, and make demands. We must be like God, adapting ourselves to the people's rhythm and their way of acting and transmitting life.

Pedagogically, this form of activism can be disastrous. By rushing people and processes it not only makes their formation difficult, but can destroy and "burn" many of them; others might withdraw, and it will be very difficult to get them back. In any case, given the apparent failure of their programs, activists easily fall into the temptation of discouragement, after experiencing the demon of impatience in ministry. "Here…with this people…nothing can be accomplished." Impatience and discouragement are twins. Both are children of pride, self-sufficiency, and forgetting that "neither the one who plants nor the one who waters is anything, but only God, who causes the growth" (1 Cor 3:7).

MAKING A FARCE OUT OF TRUSTING GOD

The principal characteristic of this demon of the apostolate is obviously to forget that distrust in oneself accompanied by a total trust in God is the essence of a minister's spirituality. The temptation here is to put trust in God in second place, as a recourse in times of need and for serious cases and emergencies, forgetting to trust the Lord in ordinary daily ministries. By not putting our trust in God with the soul's complete conviction, we are placing trust in ourselves, although we might tell ourselves the opposite. When dealing with the far-reaching and theological fruits of evangelization (the kingdom of grace), and not merely with psychological results due to purely human influence, there can only be absolute trust in the Lord and absolute distrust in ourselves. In ministry the two types of trust cannot coexist: we either truly trust in God and not in ourselves, or we trust in ourselves and not really in God.

Here, distrust or trust in ourselves is a theological quality and not psychological. The matter at hand is neither one of being insecure due to inferiority complexes nor of disregarding the gifts, human conditions, and Christian life that without a doubt God has abundantly given us. Human and psychological trust is desirable in ministry. The distrust we are talking about is on another level: that of the fruits of the Spirit. Paradoxically, in the apostolate an authentic trust in God imparts to ministers the psychological trust that they might lack as they come face to face with the reality of their human limitations.

Evangelizers who have placed their confidence in themselves and not in the Lord reinforce this temptation with the successes that their human qualities and influence give them. Often they do not perceive this habitual and deeply rooted attitude, blinding themselves concerning what they are capable of. Ministerial activities follow the laws of human effectiveness that is successful at first but not always tied to grace and the lasting work of God. We have known intelligent, trained, and very qualified evangelizers with many good qualities who often exercised a powerful attraction and influence. Perhaps for that reason itself, they put their ministerial trust in themselves more than in God. For a few years they shone in ministry. They were requested for retreats and conferences; they attracted priestly vocations; they had many followers. At a specific moment, some contradictions and failures arose, and almost overnight they burned out. Eventually many of their young followers fell away from the church. The groups and communities they formed did not last. The vocations that they had elicited left the seminaries. What happened? God left these ministers to themselves, implying "I am not with you" and reversing the promise that "I am with you always, until the end of the age" (Mt 28:20). They used to take pleasure in the results of their ministerial effectiveness.

We create a caricature when we do not trust primarily in God, but rather in ourselves. We resort to trusting God when we have not done what we should have done in ministry, when we have behaved irresponsibly, or when we have not prepared ourselves as we should. These moments of convenient trust are a manipulation of true confidence in God. Authentic confidence presupposes that ministers have prepared themselves and worked as if everything depended on them. However, having done all in their power—at times even heroic actions—they do not put their trust in what they have accomplished and done. Rather they confide in the power of God.

NOT TRUSTING IN THE POWER OF TRUTH

This demon is a variation of lacking confidence in God, but it has separate characteristics as a temptation.

Christian truth, set forth by Christ and handed down by the church's magisterium, presents doctrinal and moral challenges that go against the ideological current of today's dominant, secularized cultures and their ethical criteria. One can run into opposition declaring the loving providence of God. Many cannot believe that there are times to accept without understanding. It is not "popular" to assert truths such as the positive value of austerity, suffering, and the cross, or life after death. Likewise the value of chastity, virginity, persistence in marriage, or the defense of life even in extreme cases may be unpopular. Even for believers who accept them in principle, these truths are a stumbling block when they affect one personally.

In this context, the minister is tempted to vacillate. He or she may not offer Christ's truth as it is (with the necessary pedagogical considerations of timing, opportunity, etc.). The assumption may be that the truth will not be accepted and followed, or that it is inconvenient. Some truths go by the wayside or fall into ambiguity when in various ways the minister of the Word trusts more in human prudence than in the truth's force and attraction. Similarly, we fall into this temptation in formation when offering counsel, direction, hope. Instead of the Gospel's demands and its light, the minister proposes the "reasonable" advice of human experience, depriving people of the opportunity to yield progressively to the truth that sets them free.

Relying on the strength of ministry presupposes the ministers' conviction that the truth of faith and morals coincides with human growth and its greatest ideals. We must have the conviction that truth is people's authentic good, and therefore their only true happiness.

PREACHING PROBLEMS AND NOT CERTAINTIES

This demon causes confusion between different moments and levels of ministry of the Word. There are occasions when audiences expect a talk or conference to initiate discussion and raise questions for debate, conjectures, opinions and problems of the church.

Nevertheless, on the level of catechesis, homilies, and missionary preaching, it is always necessary to hand on the Christian message, which is the truth of Christ in one of its manifestations. People in this situation expect the certitude of the faith in order to renew their lives. They do not want their issues and problems returned to them without a response. They hope for faith to shed light on their conflicts and questions. The essence of evangelization is to announce a message and not problems, unless these are a starting point for the proclamation of the Gospel. Evangelization announces certainties, not conjectures or personal opinions.

There may be many causes of this temptation. Ministers may lack experience, judgment, or discernment. They may be projecting their interior state. If they themselves are vacillating in their convictions, or if their Christian life is more a bundle of problems and questions than of certitude, they will tend to transmit that to others. The old saying that "the mouth speaks from the abundance of the heart" fits ministry perfectly.

The Christian community is built on the faith, hope, and love of its members. It is not built on doubts, confusions, and shared problems.

SECULARIZING CHRISTIAN HOPE

This demon secularizes the proclamation of Christian hope. Christian hope is based on the promises of Christ, such as resurrection after death, eternal life, the certainty of his love and grace in this life. They make it possible for human beings to be holy in whatever circumstance, to live with dignity and be capable of overcoming moral evil and temptation in all its forms. By its very nature, ministry promotes this hope.

The temptation in this case consists of transmitting a message of purely secular hopes to the detriment of fundamental Christian hope. For example, the minister promotes a better social or political future, with the accompanying freedoms that men and women are searching for today. He or she preaches confidence in overcoming sickness, poverty, and other human dilemmas. Although we should strive for these legitimate human hopes, the promises of Christ do not guarantee them in this life. We do not know with certainty if they will be achieved. To proclaim them as Christian hope deceives the people, and reduces the Gospel to a message of legitimate human liberation or optimism about the future. This is not foreign to ministry, but it does not have the certitude of Christian hope.

To secularize hope is to do away with the proclamation of the human vocation to eternal life, holiness, faith, and love as the driving force and the supreme value of human liberation. With that, ministers will be tempted to change their service into the inspiration of secular expectations and the commitment to a better future. These are good things that challenge Christianity, but they should not replace what most properly belongs to it: the proclamation of Christ as the true hope of the human race.

LOSING A FEEL FOR PERSONS

This demon changes the minister into an executive director of pastoral work.

Some positions and jobs lend themselves to this more than others. In every case, the gradual and sometimes imperceptible result happens in the same way. Ministers become so absorbed in administration, supervision, planning, and organization that they no longer have adequate time to dedicate themselves to the people for whom they are working. Above all, their limited psychological space impedes being close to the ones they are serving.

The demon of apostolic depersonalization makes pastoral agents so dedicated to the means of action and service that they forget the people whom they serve. Organization and program proposals absorb them.

This temptation can take other forms. In effect, ministers who become "pastoral executives" will tend to place excessive importance on programs and courses of action. They impose plans on the people instead of adapting programs to their reality—the reality from which the ministerial "executives" have progressively distanced themselves. People, with their possibilities and their limitations, are the point of departure for every ministry, no matter how excellent and ideal the plans might be. These ministers forget that the people should be the ones to carry this work to completion.

PREFERRING SOME PEOPLE OVER OTHERS

Hardly anyone escapes this demon. It is not easy to become aware of this temptation. Even the spiritual minister suffers from it unknowingly because of spiritual blindness. The expulsion of this demon, therefore, ordinarily requires a lifetime of bringing to light one's apostolic motivations.

Unless this temptation has fallen to the basest levels, it usually does not involve preference or discrimination against people on the basis of serious prejudice: racism, classism, nationalism, treating the rich differently from the poor, etc. Discrimination at this level is not ordinarily found in the ministry of the church, except in unusual cases. The demon of personal preference customarily arises more subtly.

The issue here is one of giving more time, taking more interest, and being more available to people and to members of the Christian community who have better human qualities: those who are more intelligent, more interesting and entertaining, more pleasant and attractive. Subtly relegated to second place, by contrast, are those who are less gifted: those who are dull, bland, less intelligent, and less attractive and charming. This is the most common form of personal preference in ministry. The more subtle, deep-seated, and persistent it is, the more unconscious it tends to be.

In ministry, the option for the poor should not be restricted to the sociological level, which is always essential. It should reach out as well to the "poor" in external human qualities, such as those who are psychologically discriminated against in receiving care. Ministry should not be guided only by the criterion of effectiveness, which seeks to invest preferentially in the highly gifted and those who have potential for leadership. It should give equal witness to the primacy of fraternal charity, which prefers the shunned and forgotten.

SECTARIANISM

The demon of sectarianism leads ministers to become confined within their field of work, their ideas, and their unique group. In this way, they lose the sense of belonging to and being integrated into the wider, more richly diverse and universal church with which all Christians are in solidarity. They lose the sense of sharing in its successes, crosses, problems, and achievements, within their country and throughout the world. Sectarian ministers lock themselves up in the limitations of their experience, and see and judge the church through their vision of things, which has ceased being truly catholic.

Sectarianism has personal and communal symptoms. On the personal level, one of the most typical is isolation. These ministers work alone, without integrating themselves into a common mission. They do not attend meetings geared toward this purpose, or workshops for renewing and refining skills. They have no interest in joining in common plans and goals, or in periods of evaluation and revision, nor do they seek to keep in touch with other evangelizers.

As a consequence, "sectarians" isolate their work from others. They do "their thing" and have "their people," their particular experience, their vision of ministry. Anything different from their vision and experience is questionable to them: they see only faults and defects. They criticize and ignore the pastoral authority of the church if it does not agree with their vision and ideas.

Another symptom of this temptation is to limit ministry to only one area of interest (or only a few) and specifically delineated pastoral goals, such as prayer groups, human rights, liturgy, or youth ministry. Sectarian ministers have no interest in anything else. This sectarianism does not mean that there are not evangelizers in specialized fields, but what is characteristic of the good specialist is to have a broad and shared vision at the same time.

Limited pastoral vision makes ministers sectarian regarding the people to whom they direct their services. If ministers address only a single issue, their audience will become involved in only one concern as well. These ministers will always be speaking to the same audience, which shares their vision and limited interests. That leads to the danger of creating communities as sectarian as the minister.

The demon of sectarianism can thus be communal as well. We are not dealing here with what is normal in ministry and the church. Some people find spirituality more attractive; others, active pastoral practice. Some associate with their age group. Each group in its way forms teams with common work goals, Christian life, or friendship. This is not sectarianism, although every group with kindred ideas should know that it risks exposing itself to this temptation. Communal sectarianism consists of being locked into the theological, pastoral, and spiritual ideas of the group or movement. The members think they have the better truth or the whole truth, and have little to gain from other groups or movements in the church. They believe their orientation to be a privileged one. This type of "sectarianism" makes them definite proselytizers, ignoring legitimate pluralism. They are not integrated with other movements in common tasks. They ordinarily have their private agenda. The temptation can subtly lead them to make their spirituality, pastoral practice, or theology—in and of themselves legitimate—into an ideology, whether conservative, progressive, or of some other kind.

BEING LOCKED INTO ONE'S OWN EXPERIENCE

This demon does not have the same gravity as the demon of sectarianism. The temptation is more benign and subtle. It consists primarily in elevating personal ministerial experiences to the category of a universal principle. If one or another experience has been good, then everyone who works in this type of ministry ought to do it as well. If the experience has been bad, no one must do it; and if we find ourselves in a position of authority, we try to suppress it.

The temptation lies in forgetting that every pastoral experience is relative, with its particular circumstances, its own evangelizers and people involved, its own unrepeatable time and place. Therefore, just because there was no decisive outcome at a given moment, with certain people, and in a specific set of circumstances, does not mean that it cannot come about with different circumstances and protagonists.

Over the years, this temptation notably intensifies, since by then these ministers will have had a number of frustrating and unsuccessful experiences. They will tend to entrench themselves and only promote what turned out positively, not trusting other experiences and initiatives.

True wisdom, on the other hand, consists in not letting ourselves be conditioned by the successes or failures of our experiences. We must be open to the experiences of others and to trying other forms of ministry.

HOPING FOR A SATISFYING CAREER
FROM MINISTRY

This is a very active demon in ministry. The church's ministry is highly organized and hierarchical, as logically happens in every human institution that has a mission to carry out. Therefore, in the church there are responsibilities and tasks of greater authority than others, or greater prestige and power. There are also titles and external honors. The church maintains these with prudent realism and consideration for the human condition. The temptation is to identify ministry with an ecclesiastical career, and the importance and lasting effectiveness with the position held.

The demon of worldly satisfactions can tempt in a variety of ways. The crudest way is joining ministry to monetary gains. In practice if not in principle, it makes ministry a lucrative profession, though more idealistic and generous than others. (Working and earning a living in full-time ministry, without the desire for wealth, is something altogether different.) When this temptation becomes worse, ministry takes on the appearance of a business. Although it might not be "business" in the strict sense, it is enough so that it loses all credibility. This tendency can lead to being interested only in apostolic endeavors that pay, losing the sense of gratuitousness in service and evangelization.

A more subtle temptation is to hope for recognition and even praise from the laity and hierarchy of the church. Those who fall into this temptation become dependent on this type of human gratification in order to maintain a high level of enthusiasm and morale. It seems that in ministry they are not striving to please God, but men and women. When praises and explicit recognition are missing, they interpret it as ingratitude and a lack of appreciation. They begin to flag in their motivation and dedication. In a similar way, when the people with whom they work or the church's hierarchy criticize anything, these ministers feel rejected and persecuted. After a while they leave their job.

Perhaps the most subtle demon is the desire for positions and responsibilities, and the need for every change in ministry to mean a promotion as well. There is a hidden expectation of "moving up." If ministers characterized by this temptation are not promoted in due time, they resent it and sometimes "break down." This subtle demon usually disguises itself as "an angel of light" (2 Cor 11:14). It conceals ambition for promotions and positions with the excuse of striving for a more effective ministry and service to the church. The "career" often subconsciously becomes a factor in ministry, and promotion a constant reference point. This temptation results in imperfect motivations: ministers are interested in "looking good" and "winning points," and not merely serving the church freely and following Christ in poverty. The temptation also produces a lack of freedom in ministry and a preoccupation with the ministers' image. They avoid dissent and legitimate opposition to authority—which at times may be a duty in ministry—not out of a sense of loyalty, but rather in the interest of ingratiating themselves and appearing unquestioning.

LOSING THE JOY OF MINISTRY

This demon transforms evangelization into a routine and duty. On the contrary, spreading the Good News ought to be the principal source of joy for the minister. Collaborating in the coming of God's kingdom and working in the vineyard of the Lord should be a constant experience of happiness and inner fulfillment for the minister.

The parable of the hired workers who come to the vineyard early in the day and the others who come later (Mt 20:1ff) illustrates this temptation. Those who worked the entire day complain that their pay is the same as those who worked only an hour. They had not understood that the wage was unimportant. Neither was it an expression of true compensation for their work. Their reward and compensation were the act of having dedicated the entire day in the field of the Lord, with the joy and happiness that it produced.

Ministers in this kind of temptation make their apostolate just another job, weighed down by duty and routine. Like the workers in the Gospel who labored the entire day, these ministers work hard with dedication, but lose sight of the ultimate meaning of what they are doing. Their labor is a divine work where God acts to liberate the human condition and sow the seed of faith, hope, and love of God and others, that is, the promised kingdom of God.

In this work, ministers find joy and meaning for their life. Part of their happiness is seeing the good that God does through them. They humbly give thanks to the Lord because Christ chose them as his free and responsible instruments to "bear fruit that will remain" (Jn 15:16). At the same time, without losing their peace and joyful gratitude, ministers must also humbly ask for pardon. Due to their personal failures and lack of holiness, God has not been able to accomplish through them all the good that he would have liked. Because the ministers are not better, many people whom they serve are not better, remain unconverted, do not have hope restored.

The joy and gratitude we experience for having worked in the vineyard of the Lord should not make us complacent. We must repent and be converted from many things in ministry. The fruits of our labor accomplished by the grace of God are often mediocre because of our lack of holiness.

ENTRENCHMENT

The demon of entrenchment (sometimes justified with good reasons) corrodes in every way a minister's spirit of striving to do better. It generally, but not always, coincides with the passing of years and entering into maturity. Such ministers have found their small niche, their rhythm and way of working, rooted in their judgments and ideas. They are conscious that the ministry of the church has progressed, presenting new challenges and demands. However, they do not have the disposition to change and be renewed. They let the younger ones who work beside them do their work, but they do not allow themselves to be questioned. They might attend renewal workshops and classes, but these have no effect. They only want others to leave them in peace, entrenched in their ministry that, moreover, they accomplish flawlessly. It is even possible that they hold high positions in the church.

This temptation, which takes shape slowly and is inevitable when ministers lose their spirit, is usually combined with entrenchment in their imperfections. It probably doesn't have to do with anything very serious, but their spiritual dynamism has been held back. Under an honest exterior there is a mediocre interior. Dispirited, they do not have enough hope or confidence in God to improve. Tacitly they have made a pact with their imperfections and mediocrity, which they falsely think they cannot overcome, or at least that it is not worth the effort. They say, "This is the way I am."

This demon leads ministers to think that above all they have the right to look for compensations and to settle into comfort after a certain age. They end up being satisfied with minimum demands.

LACKING FORTITUDE

This demon weakens ministers in fortitude, something fundamental for the exercise of steadfast and self-sacrificing ministry
of great importance, in spite of all contradiction.

This debilitation and deficiency take on harmful forms contrary to apostolic vigor. In the first place it affects physical strength
and health, which, although not the least relevant in ministry (ministry depends, for example, on a person's health), is not appreci-
ated. One example is ease and convenience concerning food. Being attached to certain habits, these ministers become demanding
about the quality and quantity of meals, and when they are served.
They are incapable of giving an evangelical meaning to eating little
or nothing when pastoral service requires it. The same happens with
sleep and rest sacrificed to the demands of pastoral service. Often
there is difficulty with traveling by poorer means, such as walking or
by public transit. We systematically look for the quickest and most
comfortable way of traveling, with the excuse of being pastorally
efficient. We do not take the time to think about it since this excuse
can be valid in many cases. An excessive care for health, adopting
every form of prevention to which the most privileged in society
have recourse, can sharpen this lack of austerity and fortitude.
Other examples could be added.

The temptation likewise affects psychological strength, which
is as necessary for true ministers as physical strength, if not more so.
In this field, they need formation that includes a high degree of psychological resistance. This does not exclude being emotionally vulnerable like any normal human being. One must be strong enough
to take psychological knocks without being discouraged or broken.
That must be the attitude in the face of unjust or partial criticism,
slander, and accusations. This pertains as well to persecution and
suffering that may lead to martyrdom for the sake of the kingdom.
The aspiration of many ministers to live the last beatitude—"blessed

are they who are persecuted for the sake of righteousness" and "because of me" [cf. Mt 5:10-11]—cannot be improvised, and is vain if not prepared for and accompanied by the acceptance of trials and psychological crises with evangelical fortitude.

The temptation can be more serious if the test of fortitude comes from within the church. The "contradiction of good men and women," that is, the doubts and questions of community members, companions in work, and church authorities, is one of the worst causes of suffering in apostolic life. Ministers will need strength during times of tensions and conflicts in the church, when misunderstanding occurs, suspicions arise, and trust and kindness are lacking.

Apostolic fortitude purifies, matures, and prepares for the future. The demon of softness and fragility keeps ministers in adolescence, in a certain routine mediocrity, and inhibits the best service of the church, now and in the future.

PASTORAL ENVY

The demon of envy is a universal demon not foreign to ministry. Obviously its action among ministers does not have the devastating results that it has in politics, art, or other activities "of the world." The cases of envy within the church are much less serious, but are introduced in a more subtle manner.

The temptation is ordinarily expressed in an indirect way. It tends to find and immediately point out the imperfection of every pastoral initiative and ministerial undertaking that deviates from the normal. It snubs every notable apostolate with comments, jokes, etc. The church's ministerial sphere, like the social sphere, suffers from another temptation. It may sustain mediocrity by holding back all that excels, and above all questioning what is successful. This temptation is also experienced as cynicism in the face of tasks, initiatives, and ministers who want to live radically their call to evangelization. Cynicism is the most subtle expression of envy and its best enabler.

In some cases, forms of rivalry and latent or open competition directly manifest the demon of ministerial envy. This temptation, disguised by "zeal for the truth" or "service of the kingdom," operates on all levels. Similar expressions sometimes hide in many ways the envy of a partner's reputation or success in ministry.

This demon is active among theologians. The search for truth does not inspire every conflict or theological dispute. Personal interests commonly form part of the context and are active in pastoral work at all levels. How many times does rivalry push to the side and postpone without reason the promising projects of courageous ministers! The demon of pastoral envy makes others in ministerial projects and activities appear as a threat to one's influence. Falling into this temptation irreparably damages the ministerial relationship.

LOSING A SENSE OF HUMOR

This demon dramatizes and victimizes. For our purposes, a sense of humor consists of seeing the good side of apparently negative things, and learning to "stand outside" and look at situations that affect us, making them relative. At least a sense of humor helps to keep an even temper, not to overdramatize and take things tragically. It is not taking ourselves too seriously, whether in the position we hold, in our problems, or in pastoral and ecclesial conflicts. It is laughing in a healthy way about ourselves, our situations, and those who play key roles in them.

The demon that uproots or numbs the sense of humor progressively drags ministers down to systematic criticism, bitterness, and the victim complex that makes a big production of everything affecting them in an unfavorable way. They consider themselves, their work, their position important, and they take all this much too seriously. Evangelical simplicity disappears, and with it a Christian sense of humor.

Ministry, the church, and above all the human condition require a sense of humor. It is a human quality as well as a Christian one, recommended by the saints and by the most attractive ministers and missionaries. In the past it was always important in ministry. The same is true today.

In times of particular tension and conflict in the apostolic life—and in the life of the church in general—a sense of humor becomes especially necessary. For that reason, contributing to its disappearance in ecclesial and pastoral life is an ongoing temptation, a demon. Schisms, heresies, dissent, divisions, irresolvable conflicts, and lack of dialogue and communion are attitudes of people who generally have lost a sense of humor and who place great importance on themselves and their ideas. Without a sense of humor, any contradiction, reproval, or questioning originating in the church is high drama, a persecution. Therefore, a minister without a sense of humor is easily vulnerable and fragile.

Ultimately, a sense of humor forms part of Christian fortitude and facilitates it.

Part III
The Demons of Prayer

The good that one who practices prayer possesses has been written of by many saints and holy persons....

I can speak of what I have experience of. It is that in spite of any wrong they who practice prayer do, they must not abandon prayer since it is the means by which they can remedy the situation; and to remedy it without prayer would be much more difficult. May the devil not tempt them, the way he did me....

Whoever has not begun the practice of prayer, I beg for the love of the Lord not to go without so great a good.... At least a person will come to understand the road leading to heaven. And if one perseveres, I trust then in the mercy of God, who never fails to repay anyone who has taken Him for a friend. For mental prayer in my opinion is nothing else than an intimate sharing between friends; it means taking time frequently to be alone with Him who we know loves us.... And if you do not yet love Him as He loves you because you have not reached the degree of conformity with His will, you will endure this pain of spending a long while with one who is so different from you when you see how much it benefits you to possess His friendship and how much He loves you. (Teresa, *Life*, 8, 5)

Terrible are the wiles and deceits used by the devil so that souls may not know themselves or understand their own paths. (Teresa, *Interior Castle*, 1, 2, 11)

Remember that there are few dwelling places in this castle in which the devils do not wage battle. (Teresa, *Interior Castle*, 1, 2, 15)

PROLOGUE

For men and women dedicated to spirituality, prayer is one of the privileged areas of temptation. The "demons" of prayer are as varied as they are persistent. That's common sense. Since prayer is one of the essential sources of nourishment for the Christian and apostolic life (and for that matter for any authentic human life), its weakening or extinction compromises every aspect of this life.

If Christians are fervent, giving in to the "demons" of prayer will leave them mediocre. If they are serving in the church's ministry, they will become empty activists. If they are holy, they will cease being so. In every case, they will cease influencing the spread of the God's reign. For the demon, separating men and women from prayer sets them on the road to separation from God; separating ministers from prayer makes them sterile; separating saints from prayer destroys those who multiply God's grace.

For that reason the temptations of prayer are the most persistent, whether one is a beginner, on the way, or a mystic. Hidden behind apparently good reasons, the temptations act differently in some than in others, using the "tricks and the cunning" appropriate to the degree and forms of the individual's prayer.

NOT BEING SUFFICIENTLY MOTIVATED

This demon tries to keep our reasons for praying on the superficial level. When these are shallow, prayer becomes weak and sporadic, incapable of renewal. To renew prayer and give it a new thrust, it's necessary to renew its fundamental motivations: **all conversion or reconversion of prayer implies regaining strength for motivations based on faith.**

Insufficient motives for prayer are those of a psychological nature. Too many praying people have fallen into this temptation. Psychological needs, not faith, lead them to prayer. The psychological needs that lead us to prayer should not be undervalued—they can be a valuable aid—but they are insufficient: to feel devotion, to have desire and fervor, to cope with difficult moments that cause one to run to God, to obtain something, and so on. Once the psychological mood has changed, the motivation for prayer ceases. We abandon prayer until the feelings return. If we do not feel fervor or devotion, we do not "need" God for anything. If we do not "feel" the value of prayer, we have no interest or motivation to pray. Herein lies the temptation.

Only prayer motivated by the Word of God and the reality of faith, and not by "psychological needs," can overcome this demon. We pray out of conviction, not because of what we "feel." We do not pray in the first place in order to calm ourselves, get something, or find consolation. Rather, we pray in order to be clothed with Christ and to participate in his life.

Above all, in the face of this demon's temptation, **the ultimate, persistent motivation for prayer** and its solid foundation **is the conviction that God loves us and offers us the gift of liberating friendship**. If this truth of faith does not genuinely persuade us, our motives will remain shallow. They will be insufficient to lead us to persevere in prayer when the attractions based on psychology and feelings have vanished.

DEPERSONALIZING PRAYER

This demon consists in making prayer an impersonal although religious experience. This temptation affects many people who pray. One prays to a "divinity," to a "supreme being," to something religious and powerful. Sometimes one prays "to the air," just in case. However, Christian prayer is essentially a personal relationship. The grace of divine friendship unites us to God. Absolute poverty and misery encounter absolute mercy. In prayer we put ourselves in contact with a Person, not with a power or religious principle.

This demon introduces a very concrete temptation. When beginning to pray, some people neglect to be explicitly conscious of God personally present in the soul. For that reason, they do not enter into prayer and make profound contact with God. The experience of God is not realized. The ancient advice of spiritual men and women wisely encourages that we begin prayer by putting ourselves in the presence of God, even if it takes time to do so. The time spent in this way is already prayer.

A variation of this temptation makes prayer a religious experience centered on oneself. We practically ignore God as a person. We dialogue with ourselves rather than with God. We listen to ourselves—our plans, our good intentions, our needs, our faults and sins—and do not listen to God. This temptation focuses our attention on our personal and poor reality and impoverishes prayer. On the other hand, going out of ourselves to concentrate on God, who wants to fill us with divine plenitude without asking many questions about our poverty, enriches our prayer.

SECULARIZING PRAYER

This demon tempts in various ways that have a common element: losing confidence in the efficacy and influence of prayer in concrete history and ordinary life. That is precisely the temptation of secularization. A common understanding is that humankind already knows and manages the laws of nature and science, as well as the laws of history (economics, demographics, politics) and of the human mind (psychology). These laws more or less scientifically predict everything, so there is no longer room for any type of contingent intervention by God. With this perspective, even the believer seems to think that God put into motion a world entrusted to the human sciences in which God no longer plays a role. Thus prayer, particularly every prayer of petition (for the health of someone, for rain, for peace) would lack practical meaning. If one asks for something, it is only in emergency situations when human and scientific possibilities have run out. (Curiously, the secularized praying person often asks for miracles, and on the other hand does not trust in the power of prayer in daily life.)

Authentic Christian prayer, on the other hand, experiences God in everything, acting and directing the extraordinary as well as the ordinary. As the Gospel says, even our hairs are counted, and a bird does not fall unless our heavenly Father wills it [see Mt 10:29b-30]. However, God does act every day through the divinely created laws of nature, science, and history, without violating them. Only God can do that, as creator and sustainer of the world, Lord of all, without taking away anything's autonomy. The Christian experience is situated between extreme secularization and the opposite temptation: a God who ordinarily intervenes "directly," overriding and manipulating the divinely established laws of the world and humankind.

The demon of secularization of prayer concludes by putting all prayer under suspicion. It tempts us into thinking that to influence events, one must simply act, fight, and be committed. Those tempted in this way perceive prayer as an alienation from historical tasks and responsibilities. To them, prayer is an escape. The temptation, again, presents God as one competing agent among many in the world's course. The temptation confuses and distorts God. God is not just another (albeit important) factor in the world, in competition with other things. God is on a different level, the level of creation and providence. God as the "divine means" transcends the course of history and scientific laws. The entire visible world submits to them; at the same time God permits and wills all.

Prayer is always efficacious and influential in the contingent, because it is integrated on the level of God. It will always be in vain to understand the nature and way of God's efficacy with our human schema and references, since it would be trying to understand God's innermost reality.

NOT DEVOTING ONESELF DEEPLY TO PRAYER

This demon deceives by leading the praying person to habitually lukewarm prayer undertaken only halfway. That means the encounter one has with God in prayer is not a profound one. An encounter between two persons is not intense when the self-gift of either or both is not heartfelt. God's self-giving to the pray-er is always complete; however the person praying may fail to reciprocate.

In lukewarm and halfhearted prayer, the demon impedes the depth of encounter, keeping the pray-er's self-giving to God on a superficial level. That can happen in various degrees and ways. It happens when we do not fully "enter" into prayer, when we do not separate ourselves from preoccupations, images, distractions that we bring with us from the outside. We have one foot in prayer and the other outside. When the prayer time ends, we have prayed but we have not prayed, in that the quality of prayer has been poor. In some way, each time we pray, we must make a choice for prayer. Occasionally, praying requires that a certain violence be committed: by its nature, prayer is on a different level from our habitual way of acting and relating to one another. This habitual way is the way of the senses and exterior activity; in prayer, one "breaks" with this way, to proceed to the way of faith, hope, and love. For that reason, prayer requires suspending our tendencies according to the "flesh," and at the same time choosing to hand ourselves over in faith.

The temptation to experience and relate to God in prayer only on a superficial level weakens the ability to entrust ourselves to the Lord. Operating solely on the level of affectivity, feelings, and sense perceptions, which are good and necessary, does not suffice. Prayer must include the deepest element of self-dedication to God: handing over our freedom.

To dedicate ourselves profoundly to prayer consists of handing over the deepest part of our life to God. We reach this level when we decide between self-centeredness and charity, between sin and grace, between mediocrity and holiness. We are dealing with the freedom of the will. These factors, not rooted in feelings, but in the will, determine our being. To dedicate ourselves to prayer is to hand ourselves over to God and submit to the Lord the only thing we can: our free will.

NOT BEING INTERESTED IN PROGRESS

This demon ends up converting prayer into a routine duty and not into a life that grows.

The consensus among Christian spiritual people is that prayer involves a dynamism that progresses even to the point of being identified with freedom and the love of God. Through their experience and teaching, the spiritual masters have handed on to us the sure paths of the itinerary of Christian prayer. It begins with reflection and meditation, then becomes simpler and leaves method and meditation behind, until it penetrates the different degrees of contemplation.

Pray-ers tempted by this demon fulfill their obligation to pray, but more or less in any fashion, without being interested in progressing in quality. Prayer stagnates indefinitely in the first stages. These pray-ers grow in many other aspects of their lives, but in prayer they remain beginners. Often they do not realize it, nor does it bother them. No matter what, they maintain the duty of prayer. This attitude of dutiful prayer without sufficient love can be deadly, since eventually they cease praying altogether. Christian prayer is such that if it does not grow in vitality but remains stagnant, it ends up extinguished.

NOT NOURISHING FAITH

This demon consists of thinking that one can dissociate prayer from the life of faith, from one's state of faith.

On the one hand, the truth is that without faith prayer cannot emerge, since the motives that lead a person to pray come from faith. For that reason the believer prays, the nonbeliever does not pray. Also, although faith and prayer are not the same thing, they are profoundly related. A particular state of prayer ordinarily corresponds to a particular state of faith, and vice versa. Prayer is one of the few activities that a person does only out of faith.

On the other hand, we must cultivate and nurture faith (which is a gift from God), not only to maintain its force and strength, but so that it does not fade away and die. We do not possess a guarantee of the gift of faith. We can lose it because of our negligence. With St. Paul, we should respond to the question of how to strengthen and nourish the faith that comes to us through the word of God (Rm 10:17). In short, Christian prayer nourished by God's Word is inseparable from faith. The Word simultaneously gives life to faith and prayer.

From the beginning this conviction appears in the spiritual tradition of the church: spiritual men and women always based the strength of their prayer on constant contact with God's Word (fundamentally the Bible). Those who pray know that recourse to the Word makes prayer spring forth in times when praying is difficult.

Maintaining a prayer life that progresses requires a diligent and persevering contact with the Word of God, always interiorized, whether spoken or written. The temptation consists not so much in abandoning prayer directly, but in failing to have recourse to the Word and to become its disciple. The result will be the same: a dying faith and anemic prayer.

NEGLECTING THE HUMANITY OF CHRIST

This demon suggests that over time prayer should become elevated and detached from the mediating use of the senses. Under this pretext, those who pray leave behind the memory of and relationship with the humanity of Jesus of Nazareth. The pray-er ought to become "contemplative," arriving at the purely spiritual and loving experience of the Trinity in which the humanity of Christ is unnecessary and can be a hindrance.

This temptation would be contrary to the thinking of the church and the great mystics. None of them, no matter how high his or her contemplation, neglected to refer constantly to the humanity of Jesus, his life, passion, and death as recorded in the Gospels. History shows us that spiritual decadence and deviation coincide with different forms of false "mysticism," which minimize the relationship with the historical Jesus and as a consequence with the church's mediation. On the other hand, history also shows us that the retrieval of the humanity of Christ and his imitation according to the Gospels have supported the great reform movements of Christian life. Examples include the Desert Fathers and Mothers, St. Bernard, St. Francis of Assisi, St. Ignatius, St. John of the Cross, St. Teresa of Jesus.

The great spiritual masters, as well as the teaching tradition, remind us continually that we have access to the mystery of God only through the humanity of Jesus. In it, the Trinity becomes accessible to us. They also remind us that Christian prayer incorporates us into the prayer of Christ and his humanity. Finally, Jesus of Nazareth is not one mediation among others, which we can dispense with at some point. Rather, he is for us "the place where we experience God." (We could make the same analogy about the church.).

This temptation leads to many distortions of Christian life. False mysticism disembodies prayer and spiritual practices, separating them from life. It slowly dissolves any reference to the imitation of Christ. Transformed into an illusion, prayer is now impossible to verify through Christian praxis. Above all, this demon leads us to forget God's incarnation. We must root prayer and every aspect of Christian life in this incarnation, offered to all in the humanity of Christ, no matter how developed our spiritual and mystical experience might be.

He is the only way, the model of all authentic experience of God.

PUTTING QUANTITY ABOVE QUALITY

This demon often deceives even spiritual people. Prayer obviously requires quantity and quality. One must dedicate time, exclusive moments to prayer. The quantity of time dedicated indicates with a great deal of accuracy the vitality of one's prayer. Quality refers to prayer's depth and genuine experience of God. It involves the love and confidence in God that one puts into prayer, sharing much in common with handing over one's freedom and life.

Prayer's worth and progress depend not so much on growth in quantity as on increase in quality. Less quantity of prayer but better quality is worth more than multiplying times of mediocre prayer (superficial, hurried, as one who fulfills a task).

The temptation here consists of confusing true progress in prayer with the accumulation of quantity, neglecting the more essential aspect of quality, without which Christian life is unable to progress as it should. This explains why many people who pray and multiply prayer practices and piety do not change much in practical life and maintain grave errors. In some cases, the multiplication of practices constitutes a kind of idolatrous ritualism. They would benefit from allowing their moments of prayer, whether few or many, to be profound experiences of God.

How do we verify that the quality of prayer is improving? We experience it when prayer impregnates life and tends to be prolonged even after specific prayer times. This is growth in "the spirit of prayer." The goal of Christian prayer is not so much the times of prayer but the spirit of prayer, the life of prayer. We obtain this spirit and life when, rather than simply multiplying times of prayer, we imbue them with quality.

NEGLECTING SUBSTANTIAL PRAYER TIMES

This demon does not immediately suppress prayer, but weakens and diminishes it.

The temptation here arises from the way of assessing the spirit of prayer, which tends to devalue the moments of prayer. The result will be that in a short time there will be no spirit of prayer. The spirit of prayer requires a framework of quality time dedicated exclusively to prayer.

The temptation equally affects the way of understanding these exclusive times of prayer. They are conceived and put into practice as very brief and staggered moments of prayer, practically excluding substantial and sufficiently prolonged times of prayer. This prayer life is highly precarious. All prayer life implies a firm dedication to prayer, with regular "substantial" times: that is, profound and therefore sufficiently prolonged periods of prayer. Otherwise, it is like wanting to be fed well by occasionally eating only a cracker or a piece of fruit, neglecting to eat a more substantial meal at least once a day. People who nourish themselves in that way will become weakened and anemic.

In a similar way, the lack of substantial times of prayer leads people to a type of spiritual and ministerial anemia. They are no longer capable of progressing or overcoming life's crises and temptations. We can say that each person is called to a minimum time of prayer. If it is habitually and systematically below this minimum, Christian anemia will be unavoidable in the long run.

SEPARATING PRAYER FROM
THE TOTALITY OF LIFE

This demon removes from prayer one of its essentially Christian characteristics by separating the practice of prayer from the daily practice of fidelity. It introduces into spirituality a subtle and unacceptable dualism, converting prayer into an isolated rite, with no relationship to the Gospel faithfulness that the pray-er previously had, and no impulse to improve this faithfulness in the future.

Before and after the times of prayer, the relationship of Christian prayer with the totality of the pray-er's life is essential. The conditions for quality prayer do not depend so much on the immediate preparation, which is indeed important, but rather on the faithfulness with which one previously has sought the will of God. In prayer we find in our deepest being what we have sought. If we have looked for ourselves, we will find ourselves in prayer. If we have gone after other "idols," the presence of these idols will persist in prayer. If we have not sought God, we will not find God in prayer. Surrender in prayer extends the surrender to Christ in the rest of life.

It is an illusion to want a substitute for this lived surrender to God, which is the most efficacious preparation for prayer, assuming the habit of abnegation and renunciation, along with immediate preparation, techniques, and methods for concentration. The latter are valid only given a coherent totality of life. We pray as we have lived.

Moreover, the inverse is true: we live as we pray. Authentic Christian prayer necessarily influences us toward greater fidelity in life. It is not possible in prayer to deepen the surrender to God of our being, our will, and our freedom, without this surrender becoming projected in life, making it progressively more consistent with the will of Christ.

The temptation of separating prayer and life threatens both with mediocrity, while threatening spirituality with serious inconsistencies.

SEPARATING PRAYER FROM
THE WELL-BEING OF OTHERS

This is the demon of individualistic pray-ers: those who confuse personal prayer with individualistic prayer. Christian prayer is never individualistic. It is rooted in others' needs in the world and in the kingdom of Christ.

Christians never pray only for themselves and their own well-being and satisfaction, which is always given them anyway. They likewise pray as representatives of their brothers and sisters, especially those who do not pray and need it the most. They pray in solidarity with the human condition. This is more imperative when dealing with people for whom the pray-ers are in some way responsible: their concrete "neighbors."

For that reason, prayer always has a dimension of apostolic solidarity. This temptation introduces in the pray-ers a new form of dualism: they tend to separate prayer from service and ministry, which is another way to separate it from life.

On the one hand, the ministerial nature of Christian prayer means that prayer frees the heart for charity and apostolic service and identifies the minister with the feelings of Christ. On the other hand, prayer effectively intercedes on behalf of our neighbors and the advancement of God's kingdom. All this takes place in the human sphere through Jesus' prayer into which we are incorporated.

NOT PRAYING BECAUSE ONE IS UNWORTHY

This demon is one of the most common. At the right moment it tempts people of different spiritual levels, but more often it tempts "beginners."

The evident existential contrast between friendship with God (i.e., the practice of prayer) and the infidelity, sins, and misery of those who pray supports this temptation. They do not feel worthy to share that friendship. Prayer, then, appears to be a useless gesture and a hypocrisy. In that case, the practice of prayer is senseless for those who want to live an integrated life and not be "two-faced."

The temptation is subtly deceitful, as it appears under the reasonable guise that one must become more faithful and integrated before resuming prayer. It seems genuine, but it is not. It distorts prayer, which is for all believers: the good and "worthy" people as well as the "mediocre." Prayer is not an experience of our moral aptitude, but of the gratuitous love and saving mercy of God. What is worse, this temptation is a distortion of the image or idea of God. God is not a god who puts conditions on loving. On the contrary, God finds happiness in loving and in healing human misery.

The temptation is serious and comprehensive. It implies despair and a lack of confidence in God that progressively draws away from the Lord. The temptation is deadly: it leads to abandoning prayer, which is the one thing that can immediately heal feelings of unworthiness and lead to a more integrated life. Systematically cutting off prayer means putting oneself out of the reach of Jesus' love and liberating grace.

There is in Christianity the paradoxical correlation between the increased awareness of one's unworthiness and the increased desire and recourse to prayer.

DISCOURAGEMENT

This demon leads to the temptation of abandoning prayer because of discouragement when faced with difficulties that appear in prayer itself. The irony, furthermore, is that these difficulties are habitually normal in prayer.

The temptation is perfectionism transferred to the prayer life. Some think that prayer will be perfect if their conditions are perfect and if they have in prayer an "experience of perfection," in a human fashion. Since this experience is not possible in the earthly condition, the devil leads them to abandon what is good (in spite of everything) for what is hypothetically better.

Some people become discouraged because in time distractions overcome moments of concentration on God. Others are discouraged because their worries preoccupy them and remain with them during times of prayer. In both cases, they forget that distractions are not only normal, but they often increase because of tiredness, aridity, etc. Aridity and boredom may cause discouragement in prayer. People who experience this forget that maturing faith and persistence moved by love for God and not by pleasure invaluably assists prayer.

The precariousness or lack of external conditions for prayer discourages many. Physical illness, excessive heat or cold, and an inadequate place for praying may affect prayer, as well as outside noisiness and interruptions. One may prefer a different time of day to pray than is available. Often control over these conditions is out of our hands. If the temptation to abandon prayer emerges with the pretext of waiting to find better conditions for praying, the response to this demon should always be the same. We must persist in prayer with determination, whatever the interior or exterior concrete conditions may be, without ever becoming discouraged.

Prayer undertaken with good will, and above all with humility, is good prayer even if it has cooled off or become boring. This includes prayer in a noisy room, at an inconvenient time, or late in the day when one is tired. The pray-er who is discouraged by the difficulties and deficiencies experienced in prayer is the one who is wanting in humility. In that case, the temptations become a danger.

MEASURING EFFECTIVENESS BY EXPERIENCE

This demon again leads to discouragement. It tempts in many different ways. Their common denominator is persuading us that the real value of prayer depends on the pray-er's experience rather than God's efficacious actions that escape experience during prayer.

First of all, experience tells us that in spite of constantly practicing prayer, certain exterior defects never change. Those who pray do not succeed in overcoming the characteristics of their temperament: deeply rooted impatience, impulsiveness, or habits. The temptation leads those who pray to believe that their prayer has no value, that it is a waste of time. Furthermore, we experience not receiving the things we ask for in prayer: working out a family situation, overcoming a physical illness, a friend's conversion, success in an apostolic program. Then the pray-er wonders why to continue praying, if things keep on going the same whether one prays or not. Moreover, we have the experience of our incompetence as men and women who pray. Our prayer consistently leaves us unsatisfied. We let our minds wander, and we do not manage to deepen our prayer. Sometimes it seems that we are always clumsy and inadequate beginners who have not even learned to pray. We wonder if it's worth the bother to continue.

In any case the liberating response is essentially the same. **Our experience while praying or the results we see are not the measure of prayer's effectiveness. The efficacy comes from what God does profoundly in the depths of our soul. There we find the very source of our freedom, and our faith, hope, and love, during the times that we dedicate, perhaps incompetently, to prayer.** By its nature, we cannot experience this action of God by measuring psychological or practical results. The work of God in the pray-er is more profound and decisive than all that.

Concerning the first scenario mentioned above, we must affirm that it is a temptation, a deceit, to think that in prayer one does not change for the better. Certainly one does. The change is above all a radical change. That is to say, faith, hope, and love increase, and selfishness decreases; freedom is reoriented more and more to the fulfillment of Christ's will. In a word, prayer reclothes us in Christ. All this, slowly, has repercussions on certain exterior and character defects that are in the process of being purified. That takes time, however, and the pray-er should not be impatient, since what is characteristic of prayer is to transform from the roots up and not from the branches down. Moreover, there are certain exterior and psychological defects that take a long time to disappear, and they often do not disappear completely. God does not hurry in eliminating them, in order to help the pray-er live in humility and distrust of oneself. Ultimately, the Lord is not interested so much in external improvements as in the interior identification with Christ. Prayer is always effective in this.

Concerning the second case, we would have to say something analogous. We do not always observe the profound results of prayer. God does grant us what we ask for if it is good for us and for others, but according to God's terms and God's time, and not according to ours. God always responds, but does not habitually do miracles for us, nor grant us everything, since we do not always ask for the greatest good for ourselves and for others. Sometimes we ask for one thing and God gives us something else. We understand that. Also, God does not ordinarily respond to us immediately. Again, what is essential—that everything contributes to reclothing us in Christ—conditions the results of prayer.

In the third case, "incompetent pray-ers" should know that what they think about prayer, and their mediocre experience, do not affect the God's liberating action in the soul's center, which escapes any psychological verification. "Incompetent pray-ers" should persevere with humility, without "measuring" their prayer, trusting in the efficacy of God who acts in them.

NOT PUTTING SENSATIONS
AND FEELINGS IN THEIR PROPER PLACE

This demon distorts the place of sense perception and feeling in prayer by various means that threaten progress in every case. The temptation is present above all in two forms.

The first is to place too much value on feelings and perception. In this case one thinks that prayer is going well when one feels affect, devotion, perceptible consolation, etc. On the other hand, one thinks that prayer is going poorly when these things are not present, when one experiences dryness, darkness, and boredom instead. The outcome is that we tend to cling to what we feel, even to the point of abandoning prayer if it does not gratify our senses. One is willing to accompany Christ in his splendor on Mount Tabor, but not in his aridity and agony in the garden of Gethsemane.

This temptation makes us forget that the essence of prayer consists of the experience of faith, hope, and love. We do not necessarily feel these virtues. Likewise, they do not necessarily have repercussions on the sense's affectivity. Faith, hope, and love operate the same in consolation as in aridity, and one condition is no better than the other. For that reason, clinging to the perceptible and becoming discouraged in aridity makes no sense; all the more since having either sensory consolations or aridity is out of our hands. By overvaluing the perceptible we neglect what is fundamental: the motivation of faith and the profound surrender of trusting love.

The second temptation is conversely to underestimate perceptions and feelings and make no use of them, thinking that because sense perception is secondary, and dangerous to cling to, it is harmful. But this is not so. Sense perception and feeling, although not a permanent element in prayer, have a place in it. To underestimate their place is the temptation of angelism, since when we pray, we pray as people endowed with emotion and affect. Therefore, if these flourish in prayer, we should lean on them in our friendship with

Jesus, not to stay only with the pleasure and consolation, but to strengthen the self-surrender of faith, hope, and love. Moreover, remember that particular types of temperaments—and everyone at some point in life—can make good use of affect and the senses.

In short, it's necessary to become free concerning perceptions and feelings; neither to cling to them nor to reject them. Ultimately their presence in prayer depends on the teaching method of God. Sometimes the Lord grants perceptions and feelings to inspire us and help our weakness. Sometimes God takes them away to help us mature, purify our prayer, and grow in faith, hope, and love for God.

EVALUATING THE QUALITY OF PRAYER IMPROPERLY

This demon deceives us concerning the value of our prayer. It responds poorly to the question that the pray-er sometimes asks: "Is my prayer going well? Am I progressing?"

The temptation lies in seeking the answer to those questions by evaluating the prayer in itself. This consists in looking at the prayer that has taken place, and classifying it according to the effects experienced in it: joy, peace, consolation, new ideas, etc. The best mystical tradition tells us that none of this is decisive in evaluating the quality of prayer. The fundamental criterion of the value of Christian prayer is not the presence or absence of those or similar effects. The essence of prayer is the operation of grace in the soul through faith, hope, and love. Effects or experiences based on human psychology cannot verify this because prayer in itself is unverifiable.

What should the answer be, then? Is there some approximate criterion that allows us to judge—also approximately—the quality and progress of prayer?

The response of the great mystics is unanimous: the quality of prayer is verified outside prayer, in life, in lived faithfulness to God. Although prayer might seem to us arid and not very exciting, the solid indication of quality and progress consists of our desire and persistent effort to imitate Christ. We experience an increase in interior liberty and poverty, accompanied by growth in fraternal charity, commitment, and the spirit of ministry. On the other hand, we must revise our weak and stagnant prayer life, if in mediocre Christian fidelity we do not progress in surrendering to Jesus and in the values that he taught us. The superficial satisfaction and fervor that prayer might provide deceive us in comparison to its true quality.

DISCERNING POORLY THE USE OF METHODS

This demon consists of transforming the method of prayer (originally meant to be helpful) into an element of conflict in prayer.

By "prayer method" we mean the use of resources that facilitate the concentration of our faculties on God (reading, vocal prayers, aspirations, postures, points of meditation, etc.). A method is important, particularly during the beginning stages of prayer, and in periods of much distraction or special difficulty in entering a deep relationship with God.

The temptation here is to use the method in an untimely fashion or with poor judgment, resulting in injury to prayer. This temptation is present in a variety of ways, according to the personality of the pray-er.

One way is shunning any method to help one pray, trusting that one's prayer is sufficiently mature and a method is unnecessary. Sometimes we observe a lack of interest in a prayer method in those who are beginning to pray, which is worse. This temptation of self-sufficiency prevents the pray-er from entering seriously into prayer and savoring the experience of it. The pray-er ends up discouraged, for not humbly having recourse to a simple and adequate method, when help in connecting with God is necessary.

Another temptation consists of appreciating method, but without bothering to find an appropriate and personal method to help one to pray. Prayer methods, even those well known, are very different, and not all are suitable for every person. It is not a question of using any method whatsoever, merely because the pray-er read about it or because it is in vogue. It is, rather, being aware of what method or methods are suitable for the individual. The pray-er should use the method that fits—whatever it may be—and not other ones, although they may be very interesting. Prayer method is something very personal; to neglect that and continue using methods that do not help the pray-er is equivalent to not having any method.

A temptation analogous to the previous one is to use a certain serviceable method rigidly, when, given the circumstances, it would be more appropriate to vary the method. Common knowledge shows that frequently there are several methods that work, not merely one. One method may be more adequate than another during a particular time. We must know how to vary our personal methods. Not doing it at the right time leads, again, to using methods that do not help, or not using any method at all.

The inverse temptation exists as well, whose special subjects are those pray-ers that submit themselves little by little to a more simple and contemplative prayer. The demon here is in becoming attached to a personal method—to any one of them—and to keep using it when it is not necessary. The method is always relative, and spiritual masters tell us that one must use it insofar as it aids entering into a profound contact with God. Very often this contact is produced in a natural and immediate way, usually when one has been growing in the habit of prayer. In these cases the method is unnecessary and redundant. Furthermore, attachment to its use in these cases gets in the way and holds back the development of prayer towards contemplative simplicity in which the presence of God and love predominate. Becoming attached to the method in these cases is harmful, just as in other cases underestimating the value of method is detrimental.

There is a subtle temptation in thinking that we waste time in prayer when the activity of those who pray becomes passive, the guidance of the Holy Spirit predominates, and the prayer becomes contemplative. The temptation is that we would like to work with ideas, intentions, examens of conscience, points for reflection, etc. We would like to feel that we are "producing," and the renunciation of that in favor of the Spirit's action (in which we no longer have the initiative) seems to us a waste of time. The temptation is to persist in our plans, means, and method, not letting the Spirit lead us.

CONFUSING PRAYER WITH
NATURAL CONTEMPLATION

This demon leads those who pray to replace Christian prayer, properly so-called, with spiritual pleasures that usually help them think about God.

We are referring, for example, to listening to music that creates a spiritual atmosphere, to reading an inspiring book, to contemplating a landscape, to philosophical reflection. All those things are good, and should have a place in the life of every human being. Indeed, they often prepare a soul for prayer. They can be a good way to enter into prayer. However, they are not in themselves Christian prayer, since that always requires a personal relationship with God through faith, hope, and love. Prayer is the experience and contemplation of God, not a pleasure of the spiritual faculties and human contemplation.

The temptation consists of remaining in this pleasure and human contemplation without taking the explicit step of entering into contact with God. Prayer in the strict sense fades away. People spend time listening to religious music, reading a book on a Christian theme, preparing a celebration or a sermon. We should do these things, but in their proper time, and not during prayer. The temptation of doing the two things at the same time—contemplating beauty and praying, studying and praying—in the long run leads to cutting off authentic and profound prayer.

NEGLECTING ONE'S LIFESTYLE

Again, this demon separates what should be united for the authenticity of prayer.

The progress of Christian prayer requires certain conditions in the pray-er's lifestyle. This is a variation of the permanent relationship between prayer and life. In this case, however, we are not dealing so much with moral and interior fidelity to the Lord, but rather the way of living, working, and being organized. Prayer requires the support of a way of life consistent with it.

There are lifestyles that, though not immoral, are existentially incompatible with a serious prayer life. Besides time, pray-ers need to possess the psychological ability to lead a life of prayer. They need self-control, time for solitude, and personal discipline or organization in their life and work. They also must be capable of creating silence in themselves.

Prayer requires a minimum of organization in life, of contemplative discipline. For any human activity, freedom for concentration and reflection is necessary. If researchers, investigators, athletes, and writers must impose personal self-control and self-discipline, there is even more reason for the one searching for the experience of God to do so.

NOT MAINTAINING
THE TWO FORMS OF PRAYER

This demon leads the pray-er to be one dimensional, impoverishing prayer.

We are referring to the following. Christian prayer in general has two forms: communal prayer (which implies first of all liturgical prayer) and personal prayer. Because of human nature as well as the nature of prayer, both are necessary and complementary. Prayer in common enriches pray-ers with the communal, fraternal, and ecclesial dimension. It makes their prayer more objective—with the objectivity of the church's prayer—and thus avoids the illusions and subjectivism to which personal prayer is inclined. Personal prayer, at the same time, is what allows us to integrate in our deepest being the Word and the movements of the Spirit, consenting to God's intimacy.

The temptation here is that there are people who, for whatever reasons, can only pray (or only want to pray) in common. They cannot maintain prolonged personal prayer. These people have to recapture the personal dimension of their prayer. Otherwise in the long run the devil will attain his goal: to impoverish common prayer (which the food of the personal prayer experience nurtures), and make spiritual persons pray infrequently. (The occasions available for a present-day Christian to pray in common, outside of Sunday Mass, are very few.)

Some people can only pray in private. Communal prayer does not seem to do anything for them, and distracts them. Again, the response to this subtle temptation of individualism and perhaps illusory intimacy (which also impoverishes the integrity of prayer) is to discover the riches of common prayer. It is one thing to feel better praying alone—which is very legitimate; people should pray more alone than in common—and another to replace prayer in common. The inverse is also true. One who prays better in common should seek occasions of doing it and favor that form of prayer,

while always maintaining a personal prayer life. Avoiding the temptation of one dimensional prayer, all pray-ers must follow their vocation in the way that is best for them.

Segundo Galilea

NOT LETTING OTHER PEOPLE HELP

This is the demon of self-sufficiency.

The way of prayer is full of insecurities, illusions, subtle temptation, deceptions, and confusion. Prayer has criteria, certain principles and "laws," confirmed by the spiritual tradition of the church, bringing to mind the saying that "no one is judge of his or her own case."

For that reason, it is an axiom of Christian spirituality that pray-ers, above all in the long period of their training, need the guidance of another person who is competent and experienced. The counselor (advisor, spiritual director, confessor—the name does not matter) is of primary importance for education and progress in prayer.

In this field, the temptation of isolation means routine, lost time, stagnation in prayer. All pray-ers frequently need to be stimulated, supported, assured, and warned of the errors and temptations of their prayer.

This demon has a second and different way of appearing. It operates effectively in cases in which pray-ers live in an environment of human relationships where they receive no encouragement to practice and persevere in prayer. That is, the people with whom they live and relate do not pray, or pray very little.

The lack of an atmosphere of prayer is contagious, just as a human environment that values prayer is also contagious. This is applicable especially to Christian communities or religious communities, to apostolic movements, to parishes, to houses of formation. Creating in all these places a collective atmosphere that favors and stimulates prayer is of primary importance. The prayer life of many people depends on this.

Part IV

The Search for Happiness and Christian Renunciation (Discernment)

> Whenever the praise and glory of God would be equally
> served, I desire and choose poverty with Christ poor, rather
> than riches, in order to imitate and be in reality more like Christ
> our Lord; I choose insults with Christ loaded with them, rather
> than honors; I desire to be accounted as worthless and a fool
> for Christ, rather than to be esteemed as wise and prudent in
> this world. So Christ was treated before me. (Ignatius of Loyola,
> "The Three Ways of Being Humble" *Spiritual Exercises,* 167)

The synthesis of these two conditions of the Christian life—the
search for happiness and renunciation—has eluded many believers from the beginning, and has been considered by many non-
believers as an oddity.

Happiness. Acquiring it and delighting fully in it is essential—
perhaps the most essential thing—in a human being's vocation.
God wants this for the human creature. The Lord created us to be
eternally and fully happy in the life to come. In the same way, God
wills the happiness of the human person in this life, within the appropriate limitations of the human condition and always in a way
that does not endanger eternal happiness. Faulty Christian thinking believes God wants people to be happy only in paradise after
death, and that here on earth they must suffer and be denied earthly
happiness to deserve everlasting happiness. What kind of God
would this be? For what reason would God give humanity so many
ways to experience pleasure, whether spiritual or of the senses?

Then again there is Christian renunciation. The fact is that
Christ calls for many forms of renunciation, of self-denial, and he
commands us to take up the cross each day (see Lk 14:27, 33). Poverty, austerity, and mortification are values of the Christian way.

However, few ordinarily identify those values with earthly and human happiness. On the contrary, they seem directly to oppose such happiness and to go against the idea that God wants the human person also to be happy in this life.

Nevertheless, the compatibility and synthesis of happiness and renunciation are real. All the saints, whether canonized or not, give testimony to this. The explanation has two aspects that need to be seen separately.

The first aspect is the easier one for believers and those of good conscience to understand. Sometimes renunciation and mortification of what gives pleasure (loosely understood as "happiness") becomes necessary to avoid sin, immorality, vices, or imperfections of an interior freedom still subject to servitude. This is logical since moral servitude, whether great or small, is slavery because of its short and long term dehumanizing effects. Something that dehumanizes does not give happiness. Therefore the renunciation that we call for becomes necessary to ensure a true and stable happiness in this world. In this case, to assure authentic happiness we renounce what gives apparent and fleeting happiness.

The second aspect of the problem, more disconcerting than the first, is difficult to explain and incomprehensible without the experience of faith. This aspect has to do with renunciations, mortifications, and voluntary penances that in different degrees the saints and fervent believers undertake. Here we are not dealing with the renunciation necessary in order to strengthen a weakened will and avoid evil, temptations, or falling into vices large and small. We are considering renunciations and mortifications of legitimate earthly happiness beyond those required for practicing Christian fidelity. Some examples follow: the search for an austere life and deliberate poverty; the renunciation, occasionally or permanently, of legitimate pleasures; voluntary penance of any kind, and so forth.

How can God, who wills the happiness and well-being of the human person, ask for those things? Are they not things God created for human beings to find in them a little happiness? Is it not Christian to delight in all the legitimate things that life gives us, continually giving thanks to God for his goodness? All this is true. Moreover, it is part of Christian holiness. To lack those attitudes toward the goodness and gifts of life and the happiness and joys God offers is not Christian. Those attitudes should be alive and present in any undertaking of voluntary renunciation; done in any other way, the Christian character of renunciation is doubtful. Love for creation and grateful recognition that all is a gift from God is the underlying characteristic of the authentic penitent.

Does Christian renunciation therefore make any sense? The true answer cannot be foreign to the human vocation to happiness in this life as well, which is also the key to true happiness. The experience of the saints confirms it. In reality the answer is simple: those undertaking austerity, denial of self, and mortification find here a greater happiness. This legitimizes their renunciation for the good that God places at their disposal. The saint or the spiritual person finds here and now greater happiness in poverty than in riches, in austerity than in legitimate well-being, in foregoing a pleasure rather than enjoying it.

How is this possible, in accord with what is humane and conformable to God's will? To be Christian all renunciation proceeds from a great love for the poor and crucified Jesus. It is the love to give oneself and be identified with Jesus that causes this happiness to be greater than the pleasure foregone, not renunciation or mortification for its sake.

The joyful experience of giving something to God out of pure love, imitating very poorly the completely gratuitous gift of love God makes to us, is inexplicable for those who have not begun to fall in love with Jesus crucified. On a higher level, this is the experience of the saints and mystics, whose renunciations we cannot understand outside the horizon of selfless happiness found in their offering out of love.

Christian renunciation is not inhuman. It situates us at the heights of humanism, whose essential premise tells us that we find human happiness in love, encountering greater happiness in greater love. The love with which we make the renunciation or mortification, growth in love for God, and the happiness it gives us are the most important criteria for discerning its legitimacy and appropriateness.

Although astonishing to worldly eyes, we must conclude that to find happiness imitating the poor and crucified Christ through renunciation is in the end a spiritual experience. It has mystic overtones, in the fullest sense of that expression, as one of the heights of the Christian experience. Outside of this perspective, it is incomprehensible, in the same way that extended prayer or radical chastity is incomprehensible. This type of experience, if one has not personally had it, can create skepticism or recourse to psychologically pejorative explanations (for example, unconscious masochism).

The saints have had that experience as the fullness of love and freedom, and have given witness to it. It is not necessary, however, to go to them for such testimony. Many, many good Christians, persistently tested by the cross, have not lost—have even gained—peace of soul and happiness. We come across them many times. Anonymously, according to the measure of their grace, they have lived and understood the experience of the crucified mystics.

The Institute of Carmelite Studies promotes research and publication in the field of Carmelite spirituality. Its members are Discalced Carmelites, part of a Roman Catholic community—friars, nuns, and laity—who are heirs to the teaching and way of life of Teresa of Jesus and John of the Cross, men and women dedicated to contemplation and to ministry in the church and the world. Information concerning their way of life is available through local diocesan Vocation Offices, or from the Vocation Director's Office, 1525 Carmel Road, Hubertus, WI, 53033.